How high can you count?

1 2 3 4 5 6 7 8 9 1

1
one

Trace 1. Then write 1.

| |

Trace one. Then write one.

one

Circle everything that there is only one of below.

2
two

Trace 2. Then write 2.

2

Trace two. Then write two.

two

Circle all the things that there are two of below.

3
three

Trace 3. Then write 3.

3 -

Trace three. Then write three.

three -

Circle all the things that there are three of below.

4
four

Trace 4. Then write 4.

4 -

Trace four. Then write four.

four -

Circle all the things that there are four of below.

5
five

Trace 5. Then write 5.

5

Trace five. Then write five.

five

Circle all the things that there are five of below.

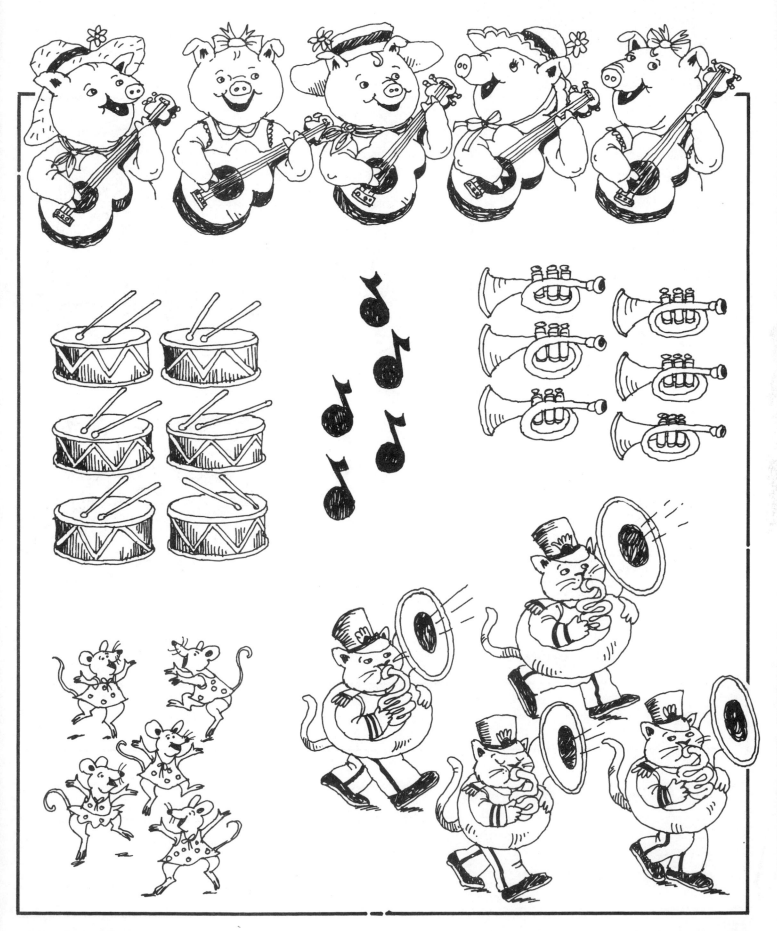

6
six

Trace 6. Then write 6.

6

Trace six. Then write six.

six

Circle all the things that there are six of below.

7
seven

Trace 7. Then write 7.

7

Trace seven. Then write seven.

seven

Circle all the things that there are seven of below.

8
eight

Trace 8. Then write 8.

8

Trace eight. Then write eight.

eight

Circle all the things that there are eight of below.

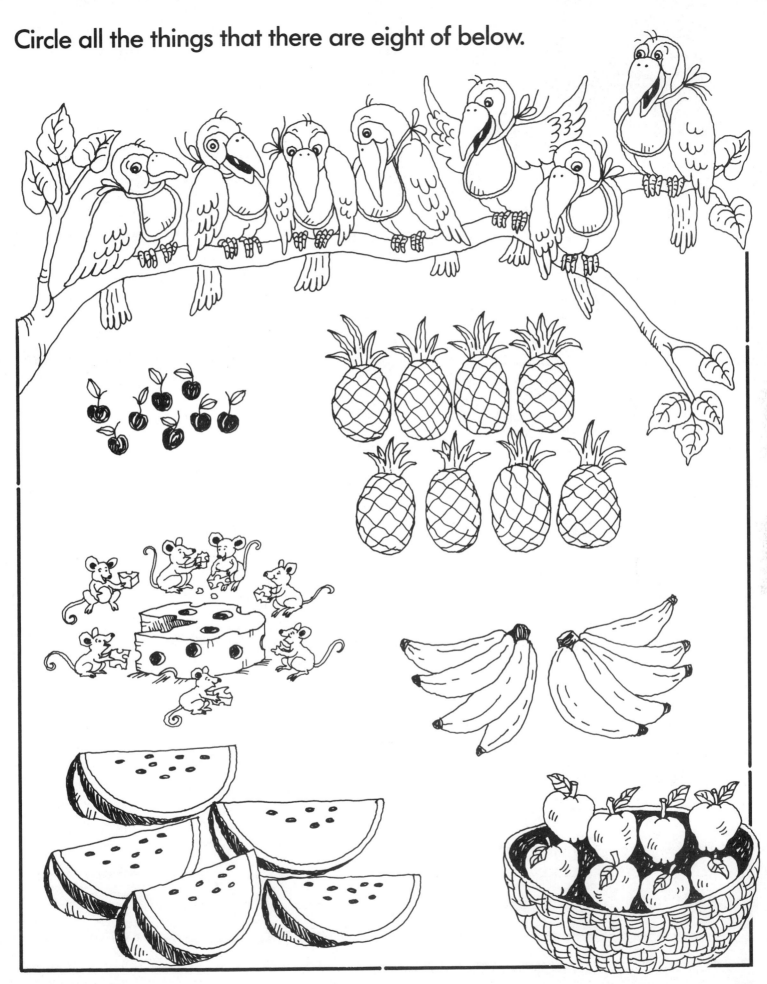

9
nine

Trace 9. Then write 9.

9

Trace nine. Then write nine.

nine

Circle all the things that there are nine of below.

10
ten

Trace 10. Then write 10.

10

Trace ten. Then write ten.

ten

Circle all the things that there are ten of below.

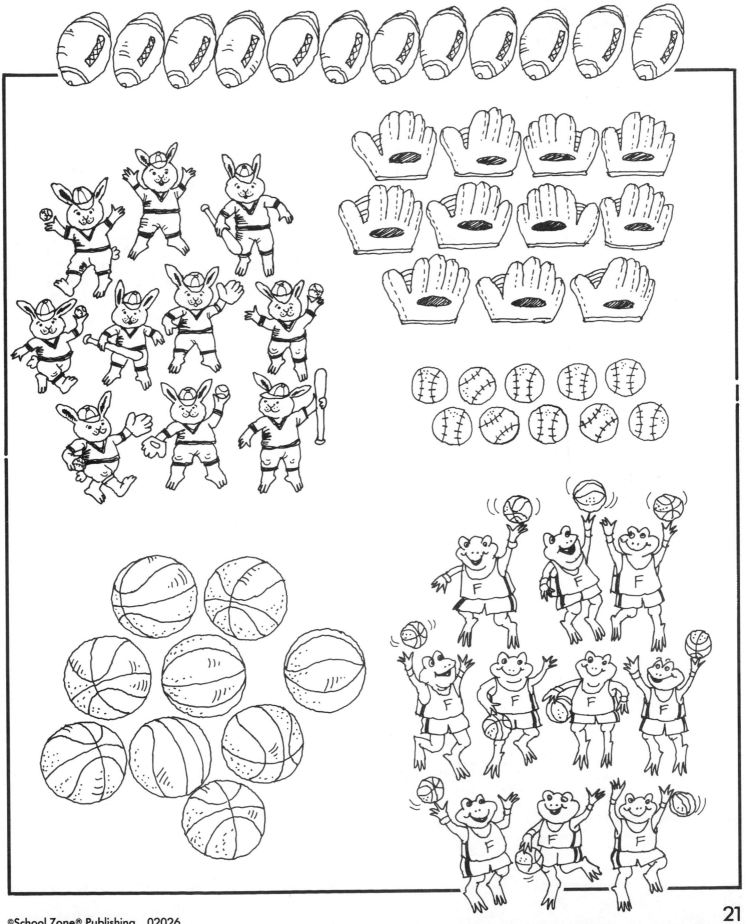

11
eleven

Trace 11. Then write 11.

11 -

Trace eleven. Then write eleven.

eleven - - - - - - - - - - - - - - - - - - -

Circle all the things that there are eleven of below.

12 twelve

Trace 12. Then write 12.

12

Trace twelve. Then write twelve.

twelve

Circle all the things that there are twelve of below.

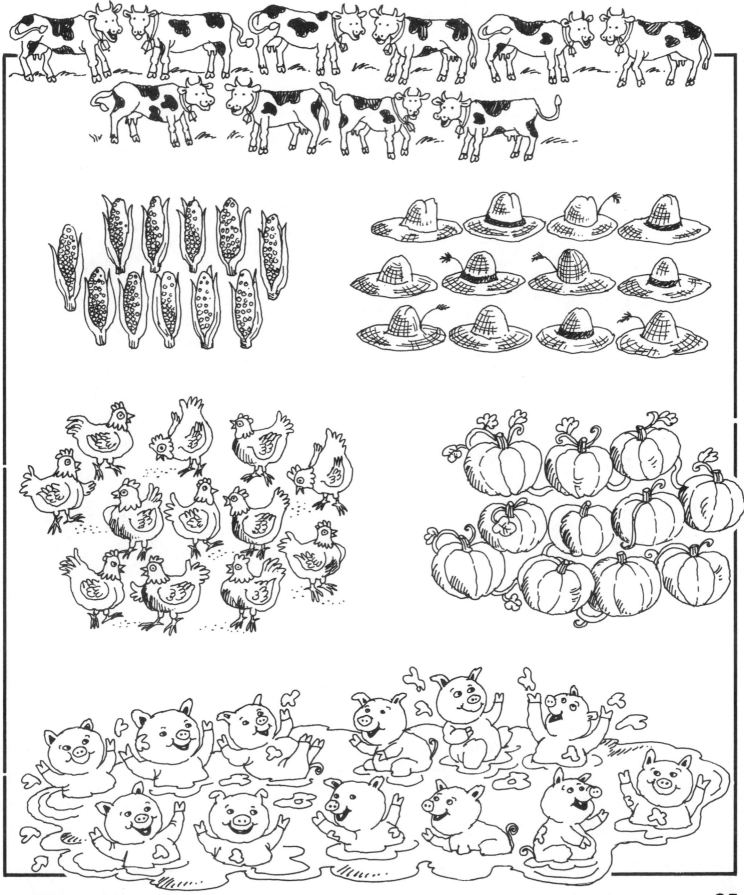

Write the correct number on each line.

How many  ? _____

How many  ? _____

How many  ? _____

26

Circle the number that is the same as the word.

three   6   7   3   2

six   6   8   4   1

eleven   12   7   3   11

five   10   5   2   4

Draw a line from each set of sheep to the correct pen.

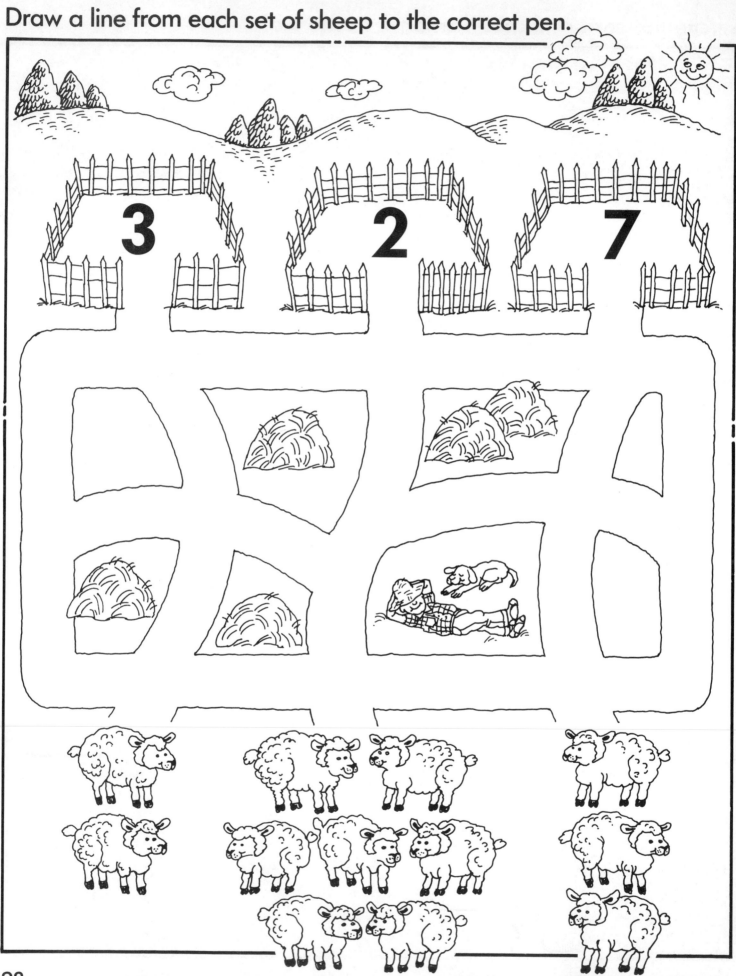

Write the correct number on each line.

How many  ? _____

How many ? _____

How many ? _____

Circle the number that is the same as the word.

four   4   3   5   10

twelve   7   10   12   1

nine   5   9   6   8

two   1   12   2   4

30

Draw a line from each set of cars to the correct garage.

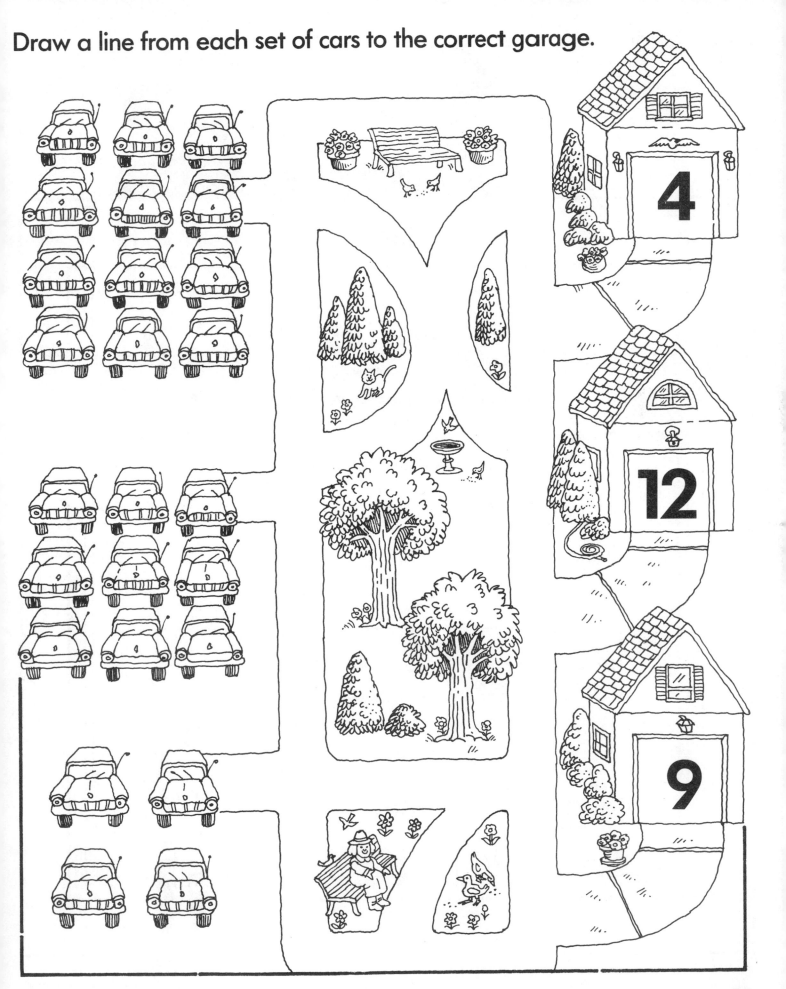

A Rhonda Rhinoceros

Award

This is to certify that

name:

_____

- - - - - - - - - - - - - - - - - - - -

_____

has completed the School Zone NUMBERS 1-12 workbook.

Rhonda Rhinoceros

I KNOW IT!

DPI